VIOLENT FAITH

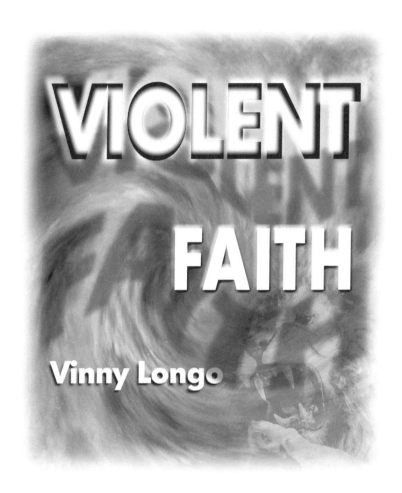

VIOLENT

FAITH

Vinny Longo

Bridge-Logos *Publishers*

Gainsville, Florida 32614 USA

Violent Faith

by Vinny Longo
Copyright © 2000 by Bridge-Logos Publishers
Library of Congress Catalog Card Number: 00-105081
International Standard Book Number: 0-88270-815-5

Published by:
Bridge-Logos *Publishers*
PO Box 141630
Gainesville, FL 32614
http://www.bridgelogos.com

Contents

Preface

Some will wonder if it is offensive to use the term "Violent" as part of the title of a Christian book in this present atmosphere of guns in America. Yet it is precisely what we need. How many campus shootings might have been prevented by a revival caused by a Holy Ghost army armed with *Violent Faith*? How much safer would our streets be today if the Church had not been tricked off the frontlines by the prevailing winds of doctrine?

Many potential voices of victory are snoozing through the most explosive opportunity in the history of the Church. Satan has labored hard to take the teeth out of our concept of faith.

In the pages of this book you will find the truth, the whole truth, and nothing but the truth. Truth that sets you free, but binds the devil.

This is not a book for those who love meetings that are light on breakthroughs but heavy on celebrating those light results. This is a manual for those who would have mountain moving, demon-stomping, delivering, miracle inducing faith.

Mario Murillo

Acknowledgment

I dedicate this book to my son, Bobby, who has gone through many rough times during his life. His faith in the Lord Jesus has brought him through this valley of the shadow of death and lifted him into heavenly places where he now has victory in his life. He is now sharing that victory with his wife, Terry, their daughter, Jessica, and son, Evans.

Out of my family, Bobby was the first one to come to the knowledge of the truth of Jesus Christ and has always in the past prayed for our family. Today all my children, grandchildren and great grandchildren are born again and serving the Lord Jesus Christ as their personal Savior. So all in the family have much to be thankful for because of Bobby's prayers. I know the Lord will keep blessing Bobby in whatever he puts his hand to do. I personally, as his Dad, would like to thank him and dedicate this book to the undying love of God that has been shed abroad in Bobby's heart.

Introduction

VIOLENT FAITH

"For whatever is born of God overcomes the world. And this is the victory that has overcome the world – our faith." (1 John 5:4)

Violent faith is about overcoming the world. The dictionary defines *violent* as "marked by extreme force or sudden intense activity; notably furious or vehement." This is the kind of faith we need in today's world.

Violent faith is the most positive, constructive power available to us. It aggressively pursues healing, deliverance, prosperity, and victory in every area of our lives. It restores relationships and sets people free from any kind of bondage.

This book shows how *violent faith* is acquired and how it is used. We give bold examples of God at work in response to *violent faith* being exercised by His people. Like our earlier book, *Victory in Jesus* (published by Bridge-Logos Publishers), *Violent Faith* helps to equip the believer with the tools he needs to wage effective spiritual warfare.

The Bible says, "Without faith it is impossible to please Him, for he who comes to God must believe that He is, and that He is a rewarder of those who diligently seek him." (Hebrews11:6) Clearly, the Christianity described in the New Testament involves a faith that is real, active, and aggressive. This is *violent faith*, and it is the kind of faith God will always reward.

We are aware of the effects of sinful violence in our society. And this makes many people afraid of the word *violent*, because the destruction caused by the powers of violence has killed so many people.

Timothy McVeigh, who bombed the Murrah Federal Building in Oklahoma City, put forth considerable energy in his effort to use violence against the government. As a result, many people, including children, were killed.

Imagine what would happen if that same kind of energy were added to the faith of believers everywhere. Satan's strongholds would crumble like the Murrah building did. His demons would flee in the face of such *violent faith*. The faith we're advocating goes far beyond wishing, dreaming, hoping, or waiting. *Violent faith* is a take-charge kind of faith that will not give up, no matter what the circumstances.

Violent faith will never accept no as an answer. *Violent faith* will not rest till the victory is won. *Violent faith* is a winning faith, a conquering faith, a confrontive faith. *Violent faith* knows no fear, because it rests in the promises of God's Word.

Every coach worth his salt tells his players that the best defense is a good offense, and that is what *violent faith* is all about. Such faith is not for wimps, nor is it for people who are afraid to offend, because *violent faith* is out to win, no matter what the cost.

This world has winners and losers, givers and takers, and victors and victims. By learning how to use *violent faith* effectively and aggressively, you will become a winner, a giver, and a victor. Isn't this what each of us wants, after all is said and done? We want to win, give, and be victorious. *Violent faith* will take you there.

Vinny Longo
Edison, New Jersey

One

God's Extreme Force

"Have faith in God" (Mark 11:22).

So just what is *violent faith?* It's a faith that produces an extreme force, characterized by sudden, intense activity in the lives of those who use it. It is power for the believer in this day and age.

Many people react to the word *violence* with violence. They react as if it is a forbidden word, worse than some forms of profanity. They do not see that there is a good kind of violence – God's violence, *violent faith* – the kind of faith that speaks God's Word, believes God's Word, and stands firmly on the solid ground of God's Word. *Violent faith* prays with full expectancy. *Violent faith* prevails.

It's also the faith of God. In Mark 11:22, Jesus tells His disciples, "Have faith in God." Here, Jesus is saying, "Have the faith *of* God." That's what the sentence literally means in the original language. Jesus is telling us to have the faith of God at work in our lives. This God-kind of faith was also proclaimed by Habakkuk, who wrote, "the just shall live by *his* faith" (Habakkuk 2:4, emphasis added.) Live by whose faith? The faith of God.

One time as I was praying about Mark 11:22, God spoke to my heart and said, "This is My faith, and I want My people to have My faith." When the Lord told me this, I began to reflect on the amount of power that is available to us when we claim and live in the faith of God.

Your faith is weak and powerless, but God's faith is dynamic and powerful. God cannot accomplish what needs to be done unless He has a willing, faith-filled vehicle. In the physical realm, God's power remains dormant until there is a vehicle He can use to release His power. This happens when the gift of faith is in operation in a believer's life.

The good news is that this faith and this power are available to every believer. They result from the anointing that comes to us because of Christ, the Anointed One. We do not receive the anointing of the Lord so we can walk around and clutch it close to ourselves, as if it has some selfish benefit or purpose; the purpose for which we have been given the mighty anointing of God is quite the opposite.

His anointing has been imparted to us so we can release the power of God into every situation that needs divine intervention. The anointing we have as believers can minister healing, deliverance, hope, and help to other people who are in great need.

The anointing of God is the power that puts *violent faith* into operation. When a believer learns how to release God's power, troubling situations lose their significance and become powerless. On the other hand, many people wonder why certain situations in their lives continue to exist – and even worsen. But it's often because they do not know the power of God's anointing,

2

they do not know how to put it to work, or they do not choose to put it to work.

Faith, Not Fear

For nearly ten years now, I've been privileged to witness God's power moving through me in our Victory in Jesus ministry, an outreach of Faith Fellowship in Edison, New Jersey. I've seen people knocked down violently as the power of God delivers them from the rulers of darkness. I have stood amazed as I've watched God deliver drug addicts and alcoholics from their bondage and on into complete and total freedom. I've watched God destroy that which has tried to rip them apart.

I've also observed people react with fear when the power of God is released. They get scared or upset when the Holy Spirit moves so dramatically through a yielded vessel. Their fear, though, is rooted in their lack of understanding of the ways of God. The power of God is an awesome thing to experience – and nothing that a true believer should ever fear.

God blesses those who walk with Him, regardless of their station in life, their stature, or their position. The prophet Micah wrote this about God's requirements of man: "He has shown you, O man, what is good; and what does the Lord require of you, but to do justly, to love mercy, and to walk humbly with your God?" (Micah 6:8).

These requirements are the same for each of us today. The prerequisite to knowing the blessings and power of God is to walk with Him daily and consistently. Amazing things always happen when we walk with God.

Walking With God

The Bible says Enoch "walked with God" (Genesis 5:24). How do we walk with God? We walk with God by faith. Enoch walked with God, and his faith was the one hundred percent variety. In fact, his faith was so strong that he literally walked straight out of this world. "And Enoch walked with God; and he was not, for God took him" (Genesis 5:24).

Now that's *violent faith* in action. That's the unleashing of God's mighty power. That's the way I want to walk with God. I want to walk right out of this world through faith. I want to please God, and the key to pleasing Him is faith. Enoch's faith was rewarded. He did not have to die; he simply vanished into the arms of God.

Each of us has the same potential to please God by walking with Him through faith. We can walk as Enoch walked, and when we do, the power of God will be unleashed in us and through us. Start with your own situation. Get your focus off of the problem and onto the promises of God. Walk with God by praising Him and talking to Him all day long. Let Him speak to your heart through His Word and His Spirit. Become aware of the Lord's abiding presence in your life.

God wants you to speak life over your loved ones and over other people. You don't have to get in their face to do this. The Word of God says, "For we do not wrestle against flesh and blood, but against principalities, against powers, against the rulers of the darkness of this age, against spiritual hosts of wickedness in the heavenly places" (Ephesians 6:12). Your battle is not in the physical realm; your battleground is not the flesh-and-blood arena. The battles you face are spiritual – and spiritual victory has a great deal to do with the words that proceed from your mouth.

Speaking True Victory

When you speak the victory that has already been won in the spiritual realm, you are speaking true victory, and you are speaking life and health and prosperity. This is *violent faith*. Because of salvation through faith in Jesus Christ, you are able to experience spiritual victory at all times.

Through faith, you are able to bring spiritual victory into the natural realm. You can speak words of life over every negative situation and every troubled individual. When you employ God's *violent faith* you can become an agent of change in every situation. Remember, it's not *your* faith that brings about the change; it's *God's* faith. That is the power you release when you speak the Word in faith.

When your child is in trouble, God wants you to speak *violent faith* into the situation. He wants you to speak life over your child in opposition to the devil's words of death. Spouses can speak life over their mates. This is true power – God's violence, which is able to overthrow kingdoms, bring the dead to life, heal the sick, and cleanse the sinner. It's the greatest power in the world.

Shadowy Illusions

To a true believer, negative situations have no real substance. They are like the "shadow of death" the Psalmist refers to in Psalm 23. A shadow is not real; it has no substance. It is, in fact, an illusion, and so are the negative situations that crop up in our lives and families. We must remember this at all times, because the devil is a master illusionist who is able to deceive the unwary.

When we learn to release God's power – His *violent faith* – in the midst of the situation or the negative thoughts, we are able to dismiss them, because we know they are the devil's lies and they have no substance. When I work with my staff at Victory in Jesus, I always remind them that it is their responsibility to shut the door on negative thoughts and to open their minds totally to the thoughts of God. As Paul wrote: "Finally, brethren, whatever things are true, whatever things are noble, whatever things are just, whatever things are pure, whatever things are lovely, whatever things are of good report; if there is any virtue and if there is anything praiseworthy, think on these things" (Philipians 4:8).

There's a time to slam the door on those defeating thoughts the enemy tries to force into your mind. The way to keep the door closed is through *violent faith* the faith of God – that refuses to see defeat or despair in every situation. When you find yourself thinking, "My son isn't going to make it" or "My husband will never be saved," remind yourself of the truth as it is revealed in the Word of God. God's Word contains the whole counsel of God, and His promises can be trusted.

Refute the enemy with the truth.

The devil is a liar; God always speaks truth. The devil is hopelessly negative; God is fully positive. The devil wants you to fail; God wants you to succeed. The devil hates you; God loves you. The devil deceives you; God leads you into all truth. The devil depresses; God exalts. The devil is weak; God is strong. The devil destroys; God renews. The devil loves evil; God loves righteousness. The devil condemns; God forgives.

Spiritual Power in the Natural Realm

When the Word is preached or read in faith, dynamic power is always unleashed. Disturbing ideas and images no longer interrupt your thought life. Your focus is God-centered, not problem-oriented. No longer will you be drifting off in your mind to places of worry and fear. Faith turns every situation into victory.

When you turn your situation, loved one, or problem over to God, your heavenly Father, He always takes care of it. God is faithful; He takes care of His property. The issue, then, becomes one of faith: Do we really believe that God will be faithful to take care of the situations we need to hand over to Him? If we really believe that, then we're able to let go and let God take control of that which is rightfully His.

God cannot take care of something until we join His faith with His faithfulness by stepping out in full confidence of the promises He's given us. He can only take care of those things that we actually turn over to Him in faith. Many people will run around and proclaim, "I believe, I believe," but when the going

7

gets tough they fall apart. A true person of faith will tough it out, because he or she knows that God has the situation and the person under control. We are so privileged to have so many promises from our Father in heaven, and yet so many people fail to recognize this.

We believe that God will do what He says He will do. He never fails.

Two

GOD IS ABLE

"Who is this uncircumcised Philistine,
that he should defy the armies of the living God?"
(1 Samuel 17:26)

Losing Hope

And a champion went out from the camp of the Philistines, named Goliath. Then he stood and cried out to the armies of Israel, and said to them, "Why have you come out to line up for battle? Am I not a Philistine, and you the servants of Saul? Choose a man for yourselves, and let him come down to me. If he is able to fight with me and kill me, then we will be your servants. But if I prevail against him and kill him, then you shall be our servants and serve us. I defy the armies of Israel this day; give me a man, that we may fight together." When Saul and all Israel heard these words of the Philistine, they were dismayed and greatly afraid. (1 Samuel 17:4, 8-11)

Dismayed and greatly afraid – a description of so many today. Just as the Israelites let Goliath's words have power over them, many today are listening to the threats of the enemy. The result is always dismay and fear.

9

The Israelites opened the door to Goliath's threats the same way many Christians today open the door to Satan's threats. When this happens, the devil gains entrance into their thought life, causing people to dwell on the worries and fears that plague them.

One giant created great chaos throughout the ranks of the army of Israel – one giant, one man speaking grandiose words that invoke fear in the hearts of God's people. That still happens today. The enemy knows what to say, and he knows the impact his words will have. He knows that there is great power in words, and he knows that if a Christian opens the door to his or her thought life great trouble can be stirred up.

The army of the Israelites looked at the physical stature of Goliath and trembled. They heard his booming voice, and they quaked with fear. Words are spiritual in the sense that you cannot see them, and that's why they're so closely related to faith, which is defined as " the substance of things hoped for, the evidence of things not seen" (Hebrews 11:1).

When the Israelites let Goliath's words in, they became fearful and dismayed. To be dismayed is to be hopeless. A person who is devoid of hope is a person who has neither hope nor faith. The only thing that can ever win against a giant like Goliath is God's *violent faith*, which is available to us through the Word of God.

Many Christians believe their situations are hopeless. This happens when they listen to the wrong voice. The wrong voice gains entrance to their thought life. It was this process that took place when the Israelites heard the voice of their intimidating enemy.

Forty Days of Negative Words

And the Philistine drew near and presented himself forty days, morning and evening. Then Jesse said to his son David, '"Take now for your brothers an ephah of this dried grain and these ten loaves, and run to your brothers at the camp. And carry these ten cheeses to the captain of their thousand, and see how your brothers fare, and bring back news of them."

Now Saul, and they, and all the men of Israel were in the Valley of Elah, fighting with the Philistines. So David rose early in the morning, left the sheep with a keeper, and took the things and went as Jesse had commanded him. And he came to the camp as the army was going out to the fight and shouting for the battle. For Israel and the Philistines had drawn up in battle array, army against army. And David left his supplies in the hand of the supply keeper, ran to the army, and came and greeted his brothers. Then as he talked with them, there was the champion, the Philistine of Gath, Goliath by name, coming up from the armies of the Philistines; and he spoke according to the same words. So David heard them. And all the men of Israel, when they saw the man, fled from him and were dreadfully afraid. (1 Samuel 17:16-24)

We live in a negative world. People seem to delight in dragging each other down through negative confessions. The media seems to set the pace in all of this, through talk shows and news broadcasts. Our world is a world of darkness.

It was the same in the time of David and Goliath. For forty days, Goliath hurled his curses, taunts, and negative words at the army in front of him. For forty days, the Israelites heard him ranting and raving.

11

Notice Goliath's persistence. Forty days is a long time. Sometimes situations come into our lives that last longer than forty days, and during that time we may be tempted to quiver and quake as the Israelites did. Goliath persistently threw frightening threats against the army of Israel, and the people began to believe what they were hearing.

Goliath had the whole army dismayed, and Satan will try to do the same thing to you. Don't let his words gain entrance into your mind. Don't entertain his words. Don't give them any credibility whatsoever.

For forty days Saul also entertained the discouraging words of Goliath – and soon all Israel joined with him. The more Goliath spoke, the more the nation trembled in fear. The power was in the words. They heard the words, and the words imparted fear to them.

Goliath was a champion warrior of the Philistine nation. His size was intimidating, and his brass armor was so heavy that no man could carry it. The Israelites shrank in fear at his frightening size, but his words did more damage than his appearance. His words gained entrance into their hearts.

David heard his words, but his response to Goliath's message was quite different from that of his fellow Israelites. They ran away from Goliath because his words scared them, but David did not.

No New Tricks

So the men of Israel said, "*Have you seen this man who has come up? Surely he has come up to defy Israel; and it shall be that the man who kills him the king will enrich with great riches, will give him his daughter, and give his* father's *house exemption from taxes in Israel.*" Then David spoke to the men who stood by him, saying, "*What shall be done for the man who kills this Philistine and takes away the reproach from Israel? For who is this uncircumcised Philistine, that he should defy the armies of the living God?*" And the people answered him in this manner, saying, "*So shall it be done for the man who kills him.*" *(1 Sam. 17:25-27)*

The devil doesn't have any new tricks. He still speaks lies to anyone who will listen. When one listens to his lies, terror and fear are stirred up. David listened to Goliath's words, but he was able to distinguish whose voice he was listening to. He immediately knew that the devil was speaking through the giant, but David was not afraid.

David recognized the enemy and exposed him for what he truly was – an uncircumcised Philistine who had no power against the armies of the living God. He had heard Goliath's words and had discerned their lack of power and their lack of truth. He looked at his fellow soldiers and spoke healing words of truth to them. It was as if he was telling them to snap out of the delusion that the devil had created through the words of Goliath.

In the same way, when the devil has someone on the run, it's important to remind them, "Who is he? What right does he have to defy a child of God?"

David had confidence in God. David possessed God's *violent faith.* David knew which voice to listen to and which words to speak. Just like him, we need to speak confidence and power into the situation by speaking the Word of God.

No enemy can stand against the sword of the Spirit. Satan is impotent against God's power and God's army.

Angry at the Power of God

Now Eliab his oldest brother heard when he spoke to the men; and Eliab's anger was aroused against David, and he said, "Why did you come down here? And with whom have you left those few sheep in the wilderness? I know your pride and the insolence of your heart, for you have come down to see the battle." And David said, "What have I done now? Is there not a cause?" Then he turned from him toward another and said the same thing; and these people answered him as the first ones did. (1 Samuel 17:28-30)

David was promised riches and honor as a reward for killing the giant, but his brother Eliab grew angry. When you start to speak the Word of God in faith and power and God confirms His Word with signs and wonders, some people will get angry at you, just as Eliab grew angry at David. Perhaps it is jealousy, spiritual blindness, or fear; but whatever the reason, some people get angry when they see *violent faith* in action. The Word of God offends them – and this is sometimes even the response of born-again believers.

Eliab tried to question David's calling and pull on his guilt strings by asking him why he left the tending of the sheep to come to the battle. He asked, "Who says you have the power?" Then he began to accuse David of pride and naughtiness.

Eliab attributed false motives to David's heart. He thought his youngest brother was operating out of pride and curiosity rather than faith. Eliab was looking at the situation from a worldly point of view.

This was not just sibling rivalry; this was a spiritual battle of eternal proportions. This was the kind of thing

Paul wrote about in Ephesians 6:12: "For we do not wrestle against flesh and blood, but against principalities, against powers, against the rulers of the darkness of this age, against the spiritual host of wickedness in the heavenly places."

Not only was David faced with this spiritual battle against Goliath, but also he now had to fight with his own flesh-and-blood brother. Clearly, Satan knew the power of faith in David, and he was now doing everything within his power to get him distracted. Satan wanted to see David leave the battlefield, and he tried to make that happen by influencing Eliab's feelings.

Eliab tried to get his brother to desist. Perhaps he was concerned about his brother, but whatever the reason, it was clear that Eliab did not want David on the battlefield, so he began to make all kinds of excuses in an apparent effort to discourage David from getting involved.

The devil uses the very same tactics today. He tries to distract us from pursuing the goals God has set for us. When it comes to spiritual warfare, he wants us to walk away, downhearted, with our tail tucked between our legs.

There are also many modern-day Eliabs in the body of Christ. They are the doubting Thomases of our times. God help them, for they will be judged for their nay saying, discouraging words. Unwittingly, they are believing Satan's lies.

David's only response to Eliab was that there was a job to do. He pointed out that the army of God was trembling before a weak, uncircumcised idolater who was filled with demons. He told the Israelites how they could defeat the enemy, but some of them didn't want to hear that. He was speaking forth what God had directed, and they refused to believe him.

David knew something that no one else seemed to understand – that God is bigger than any situation or person, including giants. Goliath had intimidated the Israelite soldiers, and they responded in fear, not faith. David, however, came to the battle scene with a faith that was determined to win. David overlooked the discouragement and distractions, and he persevered in faith. The result was great strength and authority. David's *violent faith* compelled him to speak with confidence and authority, an authority well beyond his years and his position in life. That's because God's *violent faith* is never contingent on one's status, education, or age. The same authority is available to us if we will but use the *violent faith* of God.

Ignoring the Eliabs

Eliab was also angry with David because he saw that his brother had more guts than he did. And he knew that David had greater faith than he did. The words that David spoke – words of faith and life – made Eliab angry, because his words demanded a response.

Whenever a person of faith confronts a doubter, the result is anger. We may say something as simple as, "Believe God," and this will sometimes make people angry. That's because those people don't really have faith, and to hear that they need faith is a challenge that they often don't want to deal with. The unbelieving hearts of "believers" keep many Christians in the doldrums of defeat, despair, and discouragement.

That's where Eliab was, and so were the soldiers of the Israelite army. They gave lip service to God, but they didn't really believe He would come through for them. David had *violent faith*, and this enabled him to speak with true spiritual authority. Unless your faith is up to where it should be, you will not be able to fool the devil with mere words.

David spoke with the authority that faith imparts, and he reminded the army of Israel that they served the living God. God was their commander-in-chief. God was in charge, and because of this, there was no reason to fear. Paul put it this way: "If God is for us, who can be against us?" (Romans 8:31). David and Paul were on the same wavelength, and we can get on that wavelength too. When we do, we will know with certainty that no giant, in any form, will be able to prevail over us.

Why should the armies of God be afraid of Goliath, a mere mortal? But afraid they were, and no one, except little David, wanted to fight him. All the other soldiers wanted to run. Today's army of God is so much like that. There are a few soldiers who are like David, but there are multitudes like Eliab. We must be careful to never be like Eliab – one who tries to discourage faith in others.

Eliabs say things like, "Well, you have to be careful. Think this through. Don't be foolish." Eliabs analyze situations according to reason, not faith. They are often governed by fear. Davids, on the other hand, have no fear, because God's faith has displaced all their anxieties, fears, and worries. They know who their God is, and they know He will always come through for them.

David scanned the situation through the eyes of faith, and he could only conclude that God would honor His Word. A single giant was threatening God's army. That was the cause for which David took his stand. That was his purpose, and he needed no other. He would fight the enemy in the power of God.

Notice how the devil had managed to discourage and frighten an entire army. They simply looked at the circumstances – a nine-foot-tall giant named Goliath who had a booming voice, intense arrogance, and seemingly impenetrable armor was taunting them. He must have been a frightening spectacle to behold.

But David looked beyond the circumstances – to One who was bigger and mightier than Goliath. It did not worry him that he probably couldn't have even lifted the giant's spear. David knew his God, and in simple, child-like faith, he was determined to win against all odds.

That's *violent faith*, and that's the difference between life and death in the spiritual life.

Notice, too, that Eliab was David's older brother. Sometimes it's the older, "wiser" saints of God who try to discourage you. "Don't move too fast. Be careful. God doesn't always work that way. I don't want to see you get hurt. Use wisdom."

David was ready to go and face the giant with courage and faith, but his older brothers tried to discourage his faith. Any person who steps out in total faith and reliance on God is likely to encounter "older brothers" who will try to discourage that faith.

David would have none of that. He was not about to be discouraged by his brother or anyone else.

Three

THE BATTLE IS THE LORD'S

*Then all this assembly shall know that the Lord does not
save with sword and spear;
for the battle is the Lord's, and He will give you into our
hands. (1 Samuel 17:47)*

Spiritual Warfare

Unless your faith is where it should be, you won't
know how to "pull the trigger" that unleashes God's
power and hits the intended mark. If I handed you a
weapon and showed you a target, you might not be able
to hit the target, because you were never trained in the
use of that particular weapon. The same is true with
the greatest spiritual weapon we have at our disposal –
violent faith – if we don't know how to use it.

When I was in the military service, I learned to
use weaponry that was issued to me. Along with my
uniform, the supply sergeant issued a weapon to me.
He explained that the weapon was very powerful and
that I should use it with care. I went through weeks of
training to prepare me to use the weapon that had been
given to me.

I knew I would have to qualify on the rifle range,
and I learned how to disassemble and assemble my weapon

in a matter of moments. I became so familiar with it that I could put it together with a blindfold covering my eyes. I knew its every part, and I became well acquainted with how powerful a weapon it was. I cleaned it regularly and learned how to use it most effectively against the enemy. Hours of classroom lectures, films, and on-the-job training went into my preparation to use the weapon.

Finally, the moment arrived for me to go to the rifle range in order to fire the weapon. All the schematics I'd studied had given me a head knowledge of the weapon, but I was not really aware of its power until I actually fired it. On the rifle range, I discovered the power of an M-1 rifle.

It's the same with the anointing of the Holy Spirit. I can study about it for years and never really know its power. I can even see it in action but not really apprehend its power. The anointing is our weapon, and it is unleashed through God's faith working in us.

Activated by Authority

A faith that is activated through the authority of the name of Jesus is God's faith. It is a *violent faith* that takes dominion over every situation and condition. The name of Jesus is the badge of authority that the devil and his legions recognize immediately.

When a driver is pulled over by a state trooper on an interstate highway, he or she knows the officer by a badge of authority. And, unless the driver is extremely unwise, he will obey the represented authority immediately, without questioning.

Should the same state trooper pull someone over while dressed in "civvies" and not wearing a badge, the driver will not be as quick to obey. The name of Jesus is our badge of authority, and demons have to flee when the name of Jesus is spoken in God's faith and power.

Too many believers are out of uniform. They know the name of Jesus Christ and they have trusted Him for salvation, but their lives are without authority. When it comes to a battle with the enemy, they are almost naked before him. Even when they speak the name of Jesus, they have little power because they are not operating in the power and authority of the anointing expressed through the faith of God.

Submit and Obey

If you're only in boot camp at this point, you have to learn two important things – submission and obedience. First, you must submit your life and everything you are and have to God, and then you must obey Him. The Bible says, "Therefore submit to God. Resist the devil and he will flee from you" (James 4:7-8).

The body of Christ needs to learn that this is the source of all the power that is needed. This is why training programs at the local church level are so important. We need to go beyond the boot-camp level in our training. In boot camp we learn how to be submissive, obedient, and disciplined, and we learn how to use our weapon. The need right now, however, is for believers who will go through advanced training.

You learn to fight the enemy when you are in advanced

training. You learn how to unleash God's power through *violent faith*. I sometimes look at the Scriptures in the following way: I see the Old Testament as the manual for boot camp, because it involves the law, the fundamentals. The Gospels and the Book of Acts are more like advanced training, and the Epistles lead us to the battle line. If you venture into the frontlines without having *violent faith*, the bear will eat you, the lion will devour you, and the giant will overwhelm you.

Jesus said, "Follow Me." This is what we need today: a battalion of believers who have surrendered all in order to follow Jesus, our commander-in-chief. His disciples followed Him closely for three years. They were with Him day and night. They were in advanced training with Jesus, and they learned a great deal about the anointing and *violent faith*.

We have the same anointing available to us. Jesus said, "And these signs will follow those who believe: In my name they will cast out demons; they will speak with new tongues; they will take up serpents; and if they drink any deadly thing, it will by no means hurt them; they will lay hands on the sick, and they will recover" (Mark 16:17-18).

God wants each of us to learn how to fight the battles in our lives. Until we've learned how to do this, we won't be able to help anyone else. God can't use us on the frontlines until we've been victorious in our own lives. We need to be victorious before we will be able to help others.

Rough Times Ahead

Through a pastor from Virginia who was delivered from alcoholism at Victory in Jesus, God recently warned us, Rough times are coming, and the times will continue to grow worse. Now, this warning should not come as a surprise to any of us, because Jesus Himself prophesied, "And this gospel of the kingdom will be preached in all the world as a witness to all the nations; and then the end will come. Therefore when you see the 'abomination of desolation,' spoken of by Daniel the prophet, standing in the holy place . . .Then there will be great tribulation, such as has not been since the beginning of the world until this time, no, nor ever shall be" (Matthew . 24:14-15, 21).

It is only the *violent faith* of God that will see us through the times of tribulation that are just around the corner. We have the power within us to face any adversary. We already have the victory. Satan was defeated at Calvary. You have already won. In fact, you won two thousand years ago!

Paul wrote, "I can do all things through Christ who strengthens me" (Phililipians 4:13). He also affirmed, "Yet in all these things we are more than conquerors through Him who loved us" (Romans 8:37). Now, that's *violent faith*, and that's the faith of God. Your victory is assured if you will learn to release God's faith in the face of any circumstance or any enemy that comes your way.

Violent faith firmly states, "You are of God, little children, and have overcome them, because He who is in you is greater than he who is in the world" (1 John 4:4). *Violent faith* agrees with God, who said, " 'No weapon formed against you shall prosper, and every tongue which rises against you in judgment you shall condemn. This is the heritage of the servants of the Lord, and their righteousness is from Me,' says the Lord" (Isaiah 54:17).

Many say that the end-times revival is upon us, but I

sometimes wonder if we are truly ready for a revival of that magnitude. There are churches where revival is ongoing in wonderful ways, and God's signs and wonders are following the ministry of His Word in those places. But are we ready for the final harvest?

I don't believe that the long-prophesied revival will come until God's people form a vast, unified army, one that's well-organized and well-disciplined in the face of the enemy. The army of the Lord will need thousands of well-equipped soldiers on the front lines. Most believers, it seems, are more comfortable in the support forces, somewhat secure behind the frontlines – but God's end-time revival forces will not be like that.

Those forces will be made up of Christians who are trained to win at all costs. They will know how to use both the shield of faith and the sword of the Spirit. They will be prepared to do both offensive and defensive warfare.

We'll know when revival is upon us, because folks won't be able to pass a church building without going in. They will join forces with members of all denominations and churches in an army of remarkable unity. When revival starts, God will draw all men to Himself, and most folks will be more interested in spiritual things than in material things. Won't that be a wonderful time to be alive?

God's Powerful Army

There's a wonderful chorus that conveys much truth about God's *violent faith*. The chorus proclaims, "God's got an army marching through this land, deliverance in their song and healing in their hands." This is the ideal that God has in mind for the body of Christ. We can be an exceedingly great and mighty army for the living God, and we can bring healing and deliverance wherever we go.

When we begin to catch this vision as a body of believers, the power of God will be unleashed in full measure and revival will come. But it has to begin with us – here and now. This mighty army will take back the territory that the enemy has succeeded in stealing. Broken lives, illness, addictions, troubled families, and all sorts of problems will be conquered by the power of God.

God's power, as it operates in the believer today, can stop a hurricane or a tornado in its tracks. It can stop a murderer who approaches you with a loaded gun. This amazing power is unleashed when a believer speaks the powerful Word of God over the situation.

God is calling for recruits who are willing to go to the front and be "point men" for Him. He is raising up a body of believers willing to launch an all-out assault on the enemy. This is what He is preparing us for today.

It's time to get out of the pew and head to the frontlines. It's time to take the offensive against the enemy instead of sitting back and reacting. It's time to become proactive instead of reactive – or inactive. The battle cry has sounded, and now it's time to go forth in the mighty power of God.

God won't put you on the frontlines, however, until He knows you are prepared. You must be equipped for the good fight of faith.

As we prepare to go forth into battle let's never forget that God " is able to do exceedingly abundantly above all that we ask or think, according to the power that works in us" (Ephesians 3:20). That power at work in our lives is the power of God – the anointing of the Holy One, the *violent faith* of God.

Let the theme of your life be like David's: "All this assembly shall know that the Lord does not save with sword and spear; for the battle is the Lord's" (1 Samuel 17:47).

Speaking of David

We haven't forgotten him. Much of his story also applies to the principles of spiritual warfare. Because of David's victory over Goliath, the Israelites had new faith and power available to them. They pursued the enemy and plundered their goods.

The king, however, began to grow uneasy. He noticed that his people were beginning to revere David as if he were the king. Saul grew jealous and resentful toward the young warrior. "So David went out wherever Saul sent him, and behaved wisely. And Saul set him over the men of war, and he was accepted in the sight of all the people and also in the sight of Saul's servants" (1 Samuel 18:5). The young hero was being honored for his gallantry, and people had great respect for him.

When great generals return home from a victorious conflict, they are usually honored by the people who sent them to war – the very people they protect. When General Eisenhower returned from World War II, for example, parades were held in his honor, and eventually he was elected president of the United States. The same kinds of things began to happen to David.

The women came out of all the cities of Israel, and

they began to sing and dance. At first, the celebration was supposed to be in honor of King Saul, but the adulation began to turn in David's direction. The women sang as they danced: "Saul has slain his thousands, and David his ten thousands" (1 Samuel 18:7).

This song of praise and contrast made Saul very angry. He felt greatly threatened, because he knew that the demand of the people would eventually call for David to be their king in place of Saul. He said, "They have ascribed to David ten thousands, and to me they have ascribed only thousands. Now what more can he have but the kingdom?" (1 Samuel 18:8). The Scriptures say that King Saul began to look at David with a wary eye from that point on.

The *violent faith* of David had prevailed over one enemy, but a new enemy was appearing before him. This frequently happens to people who operate in the realms of mighty faith and power, and accomplish signs and wonders before the people. Petty jealousies, fears, and insecurities all too frequently raise their ugly heads.

Instead of rejoicing over the fact that the Philistines had been defeated, Saul selfishly sought to protect his own interests. His insecurity made him murderously jealous of young David.

Saul cast his spear and said, "I will pin David to the wall!" (1 Sam. 18:11). The king began to plot the murder of his valiant warrior. Unlike the progression of events that had led David to victory, the progression of events in Saul's life led him to defeat. This is an important contrast to take note of.

Selfish jealousy led Saul to distress and depression. He began to seriously entertain thoughts of murder. Then notice what happened: "Now Saul was afraid of David, because the Lord was with him, but had departed from Saul" (1 Samuel 18:12). The presence of the Lord departed from Saul. How tragic!

David, however, kept coming from a position of prevailing faith – the faith of God. Saul removed him from his presence by putting him in charge of a troop of a thousand men. David continued to operate in the Lord's way and wisdom, even though he had been shuffled off to some remote post. The people continued to love the young leader, and "the Lord was with him" (1 Samuel 18:14). This made Saul even more fearful.

He began to plot against David in surprising ways. First, he offered his daughter Merab to be his wife. In characteristic humility, David responded, "Who am I, and what is my life or my father's family in Israel, that I should be son-in-law to the king?" (1 Samuel 18:18). But Saul reneged on his promise by giving Merab to another man.

Saul's daughter Michal then fell in love with David. Saul plotted, "I will give her to him, that she may be a snare to him, and that the hand of the Philistines may be against him" (1 Samuel 18:21). Saul tried to set David up for failure. He informed the young man that he would not have to pay a dowry for his marriage to Michal. Instead, he demanded to have the foreskins of a hundred Philistines, thinking that another foray into the enemy's camp would surely result in the young soldier's defeat. Not so however, for God's *violent faith* prevailed once more, and David arose and went forth. He and his men killed two hundred Philistines and presented their foreskins to the king.

28

The plans and devices of the godless king had no power against David's prevailing faith. Saul was compelled to reward David with marriage to Michal. Saul's anger grew into bitterness as the name of David continued to be spoken with great love and honor among the Israelites. Thoughts of murder continued to govern him, and he turned to his son Jonathan for support.

Jonathan loved David, however, so when his father asked him and his servants to kill his friend, Jonathan responded by informing David of the king's intentions. Then Jonathan went back to his father and entreated him, "Let not the king sin against his servant, against David, because he has not sinned against you, and because his works have been very good toward you. For he took his life in his hands and killed the Philistine, and the Lord brought about a great deliverance for all Israel. You saw it and rejoiced. Why then will you sin against innocent blood, to kill David without a cause?" (1 Samuel 19:4-5). The king responded, "as the Lord lives, he shall not be killed" (1 Samuel 19:6).

It looked as if Saul's heart had changed toward David, but later events proved that this was not so. God's *violent faith* unleashed in David's life kept him safe in the face of all his enemies, and it will keep you as well as long as you remember that the battle is the Lord's.

This does not mean that operating under the power of God will always be easy, nor does it mean that no one will rise against you. But it does mean that God will always be faithful on your behalf. He will watch out for you and protect you. He will fight for you.

Popularity Syndrome

A syndrome is a group of symptoms that characterize a particular disease. When I mention the "popularity syndrome," I am referring to a disease that is infecting the Body of Christ.

Many people are concerned about the entertainment aspect of contemporary Christianity. Who is the best musician? The best preacher? Which is the best ministry? Some of the attitudes of the popular culture have infiltrated the Church of Jesus Christ.

Popularity is not the issue, and entertainment has nothing to do with spiritual warfare. We are engaged in the most intense battle ever waged – the battle for souls that will culminate in the battle of Armageddon. How well we sing will not matter at that time. The persuasiveness of our speech will not be of paramount importance. Our looks will mean nothing. When the battle of all battles occurs, only one thing will matter— do we have the *violent faith* of God? The number of books and tapes we've sold will mean nothing then.

The only thing that will count at that time will be our faith. Do we believe? Are we acting on our faith? Is our faith violent enough to see us through?

Sometimes we forget how well organized Satan's kingdom actually is. It's even better organized than organized crime is. The truth is that Satan's kingdom could well be called "organized evil." Satan and his foul forces are organized in a far better manner than the army of the Lord is.

Know Your Position

God is a serious commander-in-chief. He knows the intensity of the war we're engaged in. He knows how important it is for His people to walk in the *violent faith* of His Word.

We need to know our position in the army of God just as a member of the armed services must know his or her position in order to be effective. A general who is in charge of an artillery division in the U.S. Army would likely be very ineffective as a general in an armored division, because he would not be in the place where he was trained to be. The same is true with soldiers in the army of the Lord. Like David, we need to know our position and to have confidence that God will enable us to fulfill the particular commission He has given us.

The Bible says, " The word is near you, in your mouth and in your heart' (that is, the word of faith which we preach): that if you confess with your mouth the Lord Jesus and believe in your heart that God has raised Him from the dead, you shall be saved. For with the heart one believes unto righteousness, and with the mouth confession is made unto salvation. For the Scripture says, 'Whoever believes on Him will not be put to shame" (Romans 10:8-11).

It's time for believers to get out of their compounds and confront the enemy with the word of faith. If they will do so, they will never be ashamed. When we truly understand, through spiritual enlightenment, the extent of the power of God, we will swell with confidence that will enable us to face the battle with a courage imparted by faith. We will be able to go to members of the congregation with uplifting words of truth, healing, and victory. We will be able to reach the unsaved with the power of the Holy Spirit, as revealed in Acts 1:8: "But you shall receive power when the Holy Spirit has come upon you; and you shall be witnesses to Me."

Faith is the victory. Now is the time to go forward. God's *violent faith* will conquer all obstacles and enemies.

Four

FIG-TREE FAITH

"By their fruits you will know them." (Matthew 7:20)

Faith That Destroys

Now the next day, when they had come out from Bethany, He was hungry. And seeing from afar a fig tree having leaves, He went to see if perhaps He would find something on it. When He came to it, He found nothing but leaves, for it was not the season for figs. In response Jesus said, "Let no one eat fruit from you ever again." And His disciples heard it (Mark 11:12-14).

Violent faith is an authoritative faith, which Jesus demonstrated for us in the eleventh chapter of Mark. Jesus and two of His disciples were near Jerusalem at the Mount of Olives, and He dispatched His disciples to get a colt for His triumphal entry into Jerusalem on Palm Sunday. The disciples obeyed Him, got the colt, and departed. The people of the Holy City who saw Jesus greatly rejoiced in His presence.

The next morning when they left Bethany, Jesus and His disciples were hungry. When they saw a fig tree they were no doubt pleased and optimistic. But although the tree was filled with leaves, it bore no fruit.

This caused Jesus to be angry, and He prophesied that no one would eat the fruit of that tree ever again. That was *violent faith*'s way of putting forth a curse, proving that *violent faith*, as Jesus practiced it, is able to take authority over nature. *Violent faith* can build up, but it can also destroy.

Notice the violence in Jesus' words when He pronounced the curse on the tree. This was no "gentle Jesus, meek and mild"; this was our Lord Jesus speaking with the unwavering faith and supernatural authority that was available to Him and through Him, and is available to us as well. Jesus took authority over the fig tree, and it withered away. This is *violent faith*.

Amazing Faith

Now in the morning, as they passed by, they saw the fig tree dried up from the roots. And Peter, remembering, said, "Rabbi, look! The fig tree which You cursed has withered away!"

So Jesus answered and said to them, *"Have faith in God. For assuredly, I say to you, whoever says to this mountain, 'Be removed and be cast into the sea,' and does not doubt in his heart, but believes that those things he says will be done, he will have whatever he says. Therefore I say to you, whatever things you ask when you pray, believe that you receive them, and you will have them" (Mark 11:20-24).*

Soon after the first incident involving the fig tree, Jesus and His disciples passed by the tree again and noticed that it had been dried up, from the roots upward. When Peter gave his shocked remark, Jesus simply responded, "Have faith of God." As we saw in the first chapter, this is the central message of *violent faith*.

Jesus then expounded further and told the disciples that if they only believed, they too could have what they asked of God. What a powerful prayer promise that is! It's a promise that illustrates the very nature of *violent faith.*

Jesus had the amazing faith of God. He didn't stand around and wait for the fig tree to dry up after He had cursed it; He believed with *violent faith.* Unlike Peter, therefore, He was not surprised to find that the tree had withered. He believed it would happen, and Jesus used this as a valuable object lesson for all of us.

Without faith, it is impossible to please God. Jesus cursed the tree and went on His way, believing. He knew that what He had spoken would happen. He saw the results of His faith on His return journey. God rewarded His faith. He will reward ours as well, if we will exercise the faith of God, which is our rightful inheritance as believers.

Faith is a gift of God, and it is a fruit of the Spirit. It is not an act of our will or a wish. If we will simply use the capacity for faith that God gives us, we will be walking in the faith of God. His faith always brings results.

Violent faith speaks God's Word, believes God's Word, and stands firmly on the solid ground of God's Word. *Violent faith* prays with full expectancy. *Violent faith* prevails.

When we encounter those things that we know cannot possibly be the will of God in a believer's life, we need to adopt the same attitude that our Master showed. We can speak to cancer and AIDS with the same authority Jesus used in speaking to the tree. We can tell cancer to dry up, and it will. We can speak to

AIDS with the faith-filled authority of God's faith, and it will vanish. The faith of God is within us. All we have to do is to let it come out.

Jesus gave all the glory to God, and so will we when we realize it is not our faith that produces miraculous results, but His faith alone, and His faith is at work in our lives.

That's the kind of violent faith we need to curse a fig tree, and it is the only kind of faith that works against enemies like AIDS and cancer. It is the faith of God. It is the power of God. It is the strongest force in the entire world.

Signs of Fruitfulness

But what was it that made Jesus so angry about the fig tree? Was it just that He was hungry and became vengeful when His hunger couldn't be satisfied? Or was He simply showing off His supernatural power to His disciples?

Neither. When Jesus got to the fig tree, He found it to be barren and unfruitful. Fruitfulness is extremely important to Jesus, so when He encountered a tree without fruit He was angry. Figs grow behind their leaves. This tree had many leaves, but no figs. The leaves on fig trees are usually a sign of a fruitful tree because the leaves protect the figs from the sun. But it was not so in this case. Perhaps someone had already harvested them, but whatever the reason the tree was unfruitful.

The tree was failing to fulfill the purpose for which it was created – fruitfulness – so Jesus cursed it. Similarly, when He finds people who are failing to be fruitful due to a lack of faith, He rebukes them and reminds them to have the faith of God. Only God's faith has the power to bring forth the results we seek.

The faith of God unleashes the anointing of God's power in amazing ways. God's faith may either be constructive, as in the case of the hemorrhaging woman whom Jesus made whole, or it may be destructive, as in the case of the fig tree. Whatever the case, God's faith is a powerful faith that always accomplishes miracles.

Jesus wants to see fruitfulness in our lives. We can be fruitful trees or unfruitful trees. Many within the body of Christ have lives that appear to be full of spiritual greenery, but upon closer examination they are found to be without fruit. Jesus told us this about fruit trees to make the lesson even clearer: "Beware of false prophets, who come to you in sheep's clothing, but inwardly they are ravenous wolves. You will know them by their fruits. Do men gather thornbushes or figs from thistles? Even so, every good tree bears good fruit, but a bad tree bears bad fruit. A good tree cannot bear bad fruit, nor can a bad tree bear good fruit. Every tree that does not bear good fruit is cut down and thrown into the fire. Therefore by their fruits you will know them" (Matthew 7:15-20).

Jesus cursed the fruitless tree, because it was not what it appeared to be. He cursed it to its very roots. The roots draw energy and nutrition from the soil. Jesus cursed it at its roots so that there could be no more life in it. The faith of God dried the tree to its very roots.

In the same way that David was anointed and Jesus was anointed, every believer has the right to use the faith of God under the anointing of the Holy Spirit. The power of the anointing is unleashed through the faith of God. God's faith is devoid of all doubt and questioning. It is unequivocal. It is omnipotent.

When God's faith (under the anointing of the Holy Spirit) commands, it is done! This is what happened when Jesus commanded the fig tree to dry up. It was accomplished just as the Master commanded.

Five

FRUIT-OF-THE-SPIRIT FAITH

*But the fruit of the Spirit is love, joy, peace,
longsuffering, kindness, goodness, faithfulness [or
faith], gentleness, self-control. Against such there is no
law. (Galatians 5:22-23)*

Chosen by God

Why did Jesus choose us in the first place? The
Bible gives us the answer in John 15:15: "You did not
choose Me, but I chose you and appointed you that you
should go and bear fruit, and that your fruit should
remain, that whatever you ask the Father in My name
He may give you." Jesus wants us to be fruitful.

Notice the connection between faith and
fruitfulness. Two of the mightiest prayer promises Jesus
gives us focus on faith and fruitfulness. He promises
to answer our prayers – if we believe and are fruitful.

He said, "I am the true vine, and My Father is the
vinedresser. Every branch in Me that does not bear fruit
He takes away; and every branch that bears fruit He
prunes, that it may bear more fruit" (John 15:1). A lack
of fruitfulness grieves the heart of our Lord. He added:
"I am the vine, you are the branches. He who abides in

Me, and I in him, bears much fruit; for without Me you can do nothing. If anyone does not abide in Me, he is cast out as a branch and is withered; and they gather them and throw them into the fire, and they are burned. If you abide in Me, and My words abide in you, you will ask what you desire, and it shall be done for you" (John 15:5-7).

Jesus gives us the keys to answered prayer. He stresses faith (the faith of God); abiding in Him; fruitfulness (which results from abiding in Him); and letting His Word abide in us. When we speak forth words of faith, we are speaking forth God's Word.

God's Word unleashes the faith of God into our hearts and lives. It is through the Word that we get His faith – an amazing faith and a *violent faith* – which results in miracles.

Trees Without Fruit

The key to fruitfulness is faith. The faith of God and the life of God surge through you, but unless you use it, your life will be fruitless. I see many Christians in the Body of Christ who are running here and there, enjoying meetings and blessings, and their lives look pretty good, just as the leafy fig tree did. Upon closer examination, however, we may find that there is no real fruit being produced. Our role is not to be fruit-inspectors but fruit-bearers, and at some later time, with our help and prayers, such an individual will become fruitful – but it isn't hard to discern that they aren't there yet.

Our Victory in Jesus ministry is more than ten years old, and we have seen literally thousands of sin-scorched lives come through our ministry. These victims of Satan's end-times blitzkrieg have known the horrors of drug addiction, demonic oppression, manic depression, diseases of all sorts (both mental and physical), alcoholism, broken families, sexual addictions, and other horrendous difficulties. Many of these same fruitless lives have been gloriously restored, however. The main reason they were able to find new hope and incredible victory is that they learned how to take the faith of God – *violent faith* – and release it into their situation. The result was victory – total, unconditional victory!

Trees that were once without fruit are now so fruitful that it seems almost impossible to gather all the fruit they produce. But Jesus knows, and He is harvesting redeemed lives because these folks dared to trust Him with the faith of God!

Violent faith never gives up. *Violent faith* trusts only in the Lord. *Violent faith* results in the fulfillment of God's promises. The prophet Jeremiah understood the great link that exists between trusting the Lord and faith. He wrote: "For he shall be like a tree planted by the waters, which spreads out its roots by the river, and will not fear when heat comes, but its leaf will be green, and will not be anxious in the year of drought, nor will cease from yielding fruit" (Jeremiah 17:8).

The Psalmist echoes this theme: "He shall be like a tree planted by the rivers of water, that brings forth its fruit in its season, whose leaf also shall not wither; and whatever he does shall prosper" (Psalm 1:3). The relationship between Jeremiah's promises and those of the Psalmist is obvious. God's Word leads us to trust Him in greater faith, and this brings a multitude of blessings to us, including fruitfulness, prosperity, and success.

People who have learned to release God's *violent faith* are those whose leaves remain green even when the droughts come. They have no worries in times of tribulation, because they know the victory has already been won.

Activating the Power of God

God is not concerned with a person's outward appearance. He is concerned with what's going on in the inner man, the spirit of a person. That's where the Holy Spirit resides – with our spirit. We need the Holy Spirit to help us understand the fruit and the gifts of the Spirit. We need the Holy Spirit to help us understand that God exists and that Jesus Christ died to save us from our sins. And we need *violent faith* in order to trust in the anointing that is within us and upon us.

In Galatians 5:22-23, we read about fruit-of-the-Spirit faith: "But the fruit of the Spirit is <u>love, joy, peace, longsuffering, kindness, goodness, faithfulness [or faith], gentleness, self-control.</u> Against such there is no law." Yes, faith is a fruit of the Holy Spirit, and you clearly need this kind of *violent faith* to unleash God's power in your life. Without it, you can't face the bear, the lion, or the giant. If you venture into the frontlines without having *violent faith*, the bear will eat you, the lion will devour you, and the giant will overwhelm you. With it, however, you can accomplish all things.

God's Faith Is the Power

God's faith is the power that exists within the believer, and it is only the believer himself who can release that faith to meet a given need. In the earthly, physical realm in which we live, God's power is released through human vehicles. Faith is one of the fruits of the indwelling Spirit in our lives, and we use the gift of fruit-of-the-Spirit faith to release the faith of God. God's faith is the power, and it needs to be released.

Where does this power come from? We were created with it: "And God said, 'Let Us make man in Our image, according to Our likeness; let them have dominion over the fish of the sea, over the birds of the air, and over the cattle, over all the earth and over every creeping thing that creeps on the earth.' So God created man in His own image, in the image of God He created him; male and female He created them. And God blessed them, and God said to them, 'Be fruitful and multiply; fill the earth and subdue it; have dominion over the fish of the sea, over the birds of the air, and over every living thing that moves on the earth" (Genesis 1:26-28). You and I were created to walk and move in the power and authority and dominion of the Holy Spirit's anointing wherever we go, but the devil stole this power from us. Through God's faith we are able to reclaim the authority that God intended us to have.

Fruit-of-the-Spirit faith enables us to please the Father in that it empowers us to walk in the Spirit and in the righteousness that God has imparted to us through Christ. Paul wrote, "There is therefore now no condemnation to those who are in Christ Jesus, who do not walk according to the flesh, but according to the Spirit. For the law of the Spirit of life in Christ Jesus has made me free from the law of sin and death. For what the law could not do in that it was weak through the flesh, God did by sending His own Son in the likeness of sinful flesh, on account of sin: He condemned sin in the flesh, that the righteous requirement of the law might be fulfilled in us who do not walk after the flesh but according to the Spirit" (Romans 8:1-4).

We are created in the image of God. His power and authority are within us. In order for us to reclaim and release this amazing power, our faith has to be active. Get to know the power of the anointing of the Holy Spirit.

Our faith moves God's faith, and wonderful things result when we find the bridge between our faith and God's faith.

Six

HEALING FAITH

"Your faith has made you well." (Mark 10:52)

Healing Power

In the tenth chapter of the Gospel of Mark, we read about a blind man who begged Jesus for mercy. The man wanted to see again, and he clearly believed that Jesus had the power to heal him. Therefore, he was not to be dissuaded by anyone, even those who told him to shut up. He exercised a powerful quality of *violent faith* by persevering against all odds. Jesus rewarded his faith, saying, "Go your way; your faith has made you well." And immediately he received his sight and followed Jesus on the road" (Mark 10:52). This story shows *violent faith* in action.

Jesus' anointing has been imparted to us so that we can release the power of God into every situation that needs divine intervention. The anointing we have as believers can minister healing, deliverance, hope, and help to other people who are in great need. The amazing power of the Holy Spirit's anointing is available to each one of us through faith, according to Acts 10:38: "How God anointed Jesus of Nazareth with the Holy Spirit and with power, who went about doing good and healing all who were oppressed by the devil, for God was with Him."

The anointing is the weapon God gives to each believer. It is the key to power – healing and delivering power. Through the anointing and its power we are able to know that God is with us.

What I Have, I Give You

Peter and John used God's faith and power to bring healing to a man who was born handicapped. "And a certain man lame from his mother's womb was carried, whom they laid daily at the gate of the temple which is called Beautiful, to ask alms from those who entered the temple" (Acts 3:2).

This disabled man was begging for financial assistance as worshipers filed into the temple. He was fortunate to be there when Peter and John came by. He looked at them and asked for help.

Peter said, "Look at us. Silver and gold I do not have, but what I do have I give you" (Acts 3:4, 6). What he had was something far greater.

Peter and the lame man looked eye to eye at one another. Normally, those begging for alms would have their heads down, as if in shame, but this time Peter commanded the man to look directly at him.

The man immediately obeyed, expecting to receive something from the Lord's disciple, but he had no idea what was coming. Peter used his God-given authority – unleashed by God's faith, through the anointing of the Holy Spirit – to bring healing to this wretched soul. He imparted life, healing, and victory through the authority of the name of Jesus Christ.

What Peter spoke, through God's *violent faith,* came to pass immediately, because it was spoken in the authority of the anointing. He took the man by the right hand and lifted him up. It is significant, incidentally, that Peter lifted him by the right hand, because the Bible says, "Even there Your hand shall lead me, and Your right hand shall hold me" (Psalm 139:10). God lifts us up, leads us, and holds us with His right hand, and Jesus is seated at the right hand of the Father in heaven.

Peter lifted up the disabled man with his right hand, and immediately his feet and ankles received strength! The man who had previously been content to remain incapacitated and had expected to survive on whatever alms were given to him was now able to find health and happiness in the Lord! The anointing of the Holy Spirit was on Peter, and this enabled him to command with the authority, power, and faith of God.

Peter knew the truth of God's Word: "The Spirit Himself bears witness with our spirit that we are the children of God. And if children, then heirs – heirs of God and joint-heirs with Christ; if indeed we suffer with Him, that we may also be glorified together. For I consider that the sufferings of this present time are not worthy to be compared with the glory which shall be revealed in us" (Romans 8:16-18).

We are children of God! We are heirs of God and joint-heirs with Christ. What is our inheritance? All the privileges of the kingdom of God. The Bible says, "Blessed be the God and Father of our Lord Jesus Christ, who has blessed us with every spiritual blessing in heavenly places in Christ" (Ephesians 1:3). Our Father has already blessed us with every spiritual blessing! All we have to do is walk in those blessings through the faith of God and the anointing of the Holy Spirit.

God has anointed you and me with the Holy Spirit and power! Therefore, He expects you and me to go about doing good, healing the oppressed, without any worry whatsoever, because He is with us. Hallelujah!

Get to know the power of the anointing of the Holy Spirit. Peter possessed saving faith, and when the lame man begged him for alms, Peter's fruit-of-the-Spirit faith went into operation. The next step was the unleashing of the faith of God into the seemingly impossible situation. This man had suffered from a congenital deformity that had left him disabled. For his entire life he had been unable to walk. Such a situation calls for the faith of God, and Peter was anointed with the Holy Spirit and power, which enabled *violent faith* to be unleashed.

Faith in His Name

The people who saw this healing were filled with amazement and wonder. Peter used the opportunity to witness to the crowd: "Men of Israel, why do you marvel at this? Or why look so intently at us, as though by our own power or godliness we had made this man walk? The God of Abraham, Isaac, and Jacob, the God of our fathers, glorified His Servant Jesus, whom you delivered up and denied in the presence of Pilate, when he was determined to let Him go. But you denied the Holy One and the Just, and asked for a murderer to be granted to you, and killed the Prince of life, whom God raised from the dead, of which we are witnesses. And His name, through faith in His name, has made this man strong, whom you see and know. Yes, the faith which comes through Him has given him this perfect soundness in the presence of you all" (Acts 3:12-16). Peter imparted God's faith to the lame man. He went beyond saving faith and fruit-of-the-Spirit faith, and spoke with the full authority and anointing of the Holy Spirit. This was Mark 11:22 faith in operation, and it made the man perfectly whole.

What God Has in Store

In Mark 5, we read the marvelous story of the woman who had had an issue of blood for more than twelve years. She was in a crowd of people who thronged around the Master. This woman, like so many people today, had spent a fortune on medical care, but it seemed to just make matters worse for her. She knew that Jesus was her only hope.

As weak as she was, she somehow managed to work her way through the crowd in order to find Jesus. She believed and spoke these words, "If only I may touch His clothes, I shall be made well" (Mark 5:28). Through the anointing of the Holy Spirit, she had discovered the key to releasing God's power and unleashing *violent faith* – a faith so strong that it would heal her.

The woman touched the robe Jesus was wearing, and immediately she was made whole. Jesus did not see her touch His robe, but He knew that God's power had gone forth from Him. He asked His disciples, "Who touched me?" The woman must have been a bit frightened to hear Him ask this, perhaps for fear that the Lord would reprimand her for having touched Him. Nonetheless, she fell down before Him and confessed what she had done.

The Master responded, "Daughter, your faith has made you well. Go in peace, and be healed of your affliction" (Mark 5:34).

This woman was healed instantaneously by acting on something that was implanted within her. She hadn't been taught these things. The fruit-of-the-Spirit faith was within her, but it became the faith of God when she acted on it. She knew Jesus was a man of great power, and this stirred her faith to such an extent that the faith of God that was within Jesus was automatically discharged in her direction, and the fountain of blood was dried up in an instant.

From faith to faith we grow to understand the faith of God – *violent faith* – and this enables us to be all that God intends us to be. Through the faith of God we become conquerors, victors, and champions. We become winners, not losers; we become victors, not victims. Through the faith of God we rise above the circumstances instead of finding ourselves under them. Through the faith of God we experience healing, power, miracles, and all that God has in store for us. Through the faith of God we receive answers to our prayers, and our ministry becomes fruitful. Through the faith of God we overcome all the works of darkness.

Power in the Tongue

Be careful what you say, because the power of life and death is in your tongue. Be extremely careful about what you say to God, what you say to others, and what you say to yourself. Whenever you open your mouth you give your thoughts, feelings, and beliefs away. People near you hear you, and so does the devil.

Always remember that the devil cannot read your mind. The only access he has to your mind is through your words. If you don't bring an evil thought to your lips, the devil cannot possibly know what you are thinking. God knows, but the devil does not. When you open your mouth, the devil hears you and begins to plot his next strategy against you (see Job 2:1-2).

We can speak life, or we can speak death. The choice is ours, but *violent faith* enables us to choose correctly. When an evil thought comes, speak life to it. Speak victory to defeat. Speak health to sickness. Speak hope to despair. Speak truth to every lie. Speak *violent faith* to every lie.

Parents can use God's faith to speak life over their children. Spouses can speak life over their mates. This is true power – it is God's violence that is able to overthrow kingdoms, bring the dead to life, heal the sick, and cleanse the sinner. It's the greatest power in the world.

You have to take Him at His Word. If He promises healing, believe it. Don't go around saying, "I've had such horrible pain for weeks." Every time you make such a negative confession, you cancel out the power of God's promises, and faith falls by the wayside. Stay with it, and don't speak lies. Speak truth. Speak power. Speak healing, and speak life.

"He sent His word, and healed them, and delivered them from their destructions" (Psalm 107:20).

Whose Voice Are You Listening To?

The old Sunday school chorus imparts superior wisdom when it admonishes, "Be careful little eyes what you see. Be careful little feet where you go. Be careful little ears what you hear." Listen to what is being spoken to you. Listen carefully and find out whose voice you are listening to.

Though you cannot see words, you do hear them, and they go right to your heart. When you open the door to the words you are hearing, they will find a lodging place in your heart and, after a while, you will act upon them.

Hang around with people of faith, not people of negativity and discouragement. Do not let anyone speak negative words over you, because these pronouncements become curses in your life, and curses have the power to destroy. Be with people of love and faith who care about you and believe God will do all that He promises. Be with yes-sayers and avoid all nay-sayers.

Get around people who understand the principles of God's faith. When you start to complain about something, these people will remind you of the veracity of God's Word – they will set you straight in love. Such people are true friends.

David heard discouraging words spoken by his older brothers, men he may have felt he should emulate and listen to. Thank God he did not do so, however, because his faith was rooted and grounded in the soil of God's Word. He knew His God. He knew how God had been there for him when he slew the lion and the bear, and he believed God would be with him when he confronted the giant. He didn't look at the situation through human reason. Instead, he looked at it with faith.

Through *violent faith*, David envisioned an entirely different scenario, and God rewarded him by putting His power at the young man's disposal. In the same way, when you experience the power of the Word of faith you will be stronger. You will develop courage and confidence to enable you to confront all enemies. You will no longer fear, because faith will have displaced your fear.

You will also be persistent. Persistence, perseverance, and patience are all interrelated terms. They stem from faith.

Most of the time, it's best to keep your mouth shut, because if you permit negative words to proceed from your lips, they cancel out faith. Just keep on keeping on, and keep on believing. God will come through for you no matter what the situation is. Always speak God's positive words. Speak forth His promises, because when you do, you speak forth life and fulfillment.

This does not mean that when you experience pain you should deny it. This is not a teaching of denial of reality. Rather, it is a teaching that says, "Though my pain is real, I choose to believe God. I will not complain. I will rejoice, because I know God is at work."

Humiliate the spirit of infirmity, and all evil spirits, by speaking them away from you and the situation you face. They have no right to be there, because you are God's property. Believe, believe, believe, and you shall receive, receive, receive.

Seven

IRRESISTIBLE FAITH

*"I have come that they may have life,
and that they may have it more abundantly."*
(John 10:10)

Reservoir of Power

Believers are walking around with unfathomable power within them, and they're not even aware of how much power is at their disposal. It's tragic. We all need to get a glimpse of the reservoir of power that is available to us.

Once, when I was preaching in Jamaica, a Rastafarian came toward me in a threatening manner. He reached into his pocket as if to get a weapon. As he drew very close to me, all of a sudden it was as if he had run into a concrete block wall! It was an invisible wall, to be sure, but it was a wall nonetheless. I even tried to feel it, but nothing was there. Something had stopped him, however, and he couldn't move beyond it. I know that God had built a protective shield around me. That was the anointing, and it came to me through *violent faith.*

The Rastafarian cursed, ranted, and raved, but he could not penetrate God's wall. He swore at me, but he could not get his hand out of his pocket. It was as if he had been handcuffed in a miraculous, mysterious way.

As Church members and leaders learn to unleash the faith and power of God, we will see this kind of radical power in our churches and in society at large. We will see Mark 11:22 in action before our eyes. Not only will we *have* the faith of God, but we will know how to release it as well. Then we'll be ready to be used in marvelous ways, because we will know how to unleash God's power through *violent faith*.

This is the only kind of faith that works against enemies like AIDS and cancer. It believes that you have the right to release God's power to defeat whatever enemy may have come against you.

A high priority in each of our lives must be to keep our faith level built up. If you're still sucking on a pacifier, you're not able to pull the trigger of God's weapon of *violent faith*.

Violent faith, we must remember, is an extreme force or sudden, intense activity. It is God's power being unleashed, both within and without. When a drug addict comes to our services, the anointing brings deliverance to him and he is set free. He has to remember, however, that he is only in boot camp and needs further training and development in *violent faith* before he can unleash God's power to others.

The training program in spiritual boot camp involves spending every day with God. Read your Bible. Pray. Worship. Spend time with other believers. Sit under the anointed ministry of the Word of God. Have Christian fellowship – witnessing, praying, and worshiping whenever you can. This is how faith is established, developed, and unleashed in our lives.

Vessels He Can Use

At a time when my youngest daughter lived three thousand miles away from me, she began to experience some major battles in her life – and I began to worry. I was afraid that she was going haywire, and since she was responsible for two children, my natural mind began to worry. Then the Lord spoke to my heart and said, *"You preach it; now why don't you act on it?"*

That's all I needed to hear. I was reminded to use His irresistible faith to speak His irresistible Word so that His irresistible power could be released against the powers of darkness and principalities that were coming against her. I unleashed God's power in the name of Jesus, and He was victorious over the forces of darkness in my daughter's life – even though we were a continent apart!

Now my daughter is saved and sanctified, and preaches like I do! Once, when she was preaching, a woman who was oppressed and in need of prayer came up to her. The ushers told the woman to sit down, because they were afraid she would demand too much of my daughter's time. My daughter, noticing the commotion, called the woman to come up for ministry. She knew she had to take care of God's business first.

As my daughter ministered to the oppressed woman, the woman fell under the power of the Holy Spirit and lay there for a half-hour. When she got up, she was a delivered woman!

Those are the kinds of wonderful things that happen when we take God at His Word and use the *violent faith* He has imparted to us. In learning to use it, we need to remember that it involves releasing His irresistible faith against the powers of darkness and the principalities of the air. The modifier *irresistible* means that God's faith, Word, and power cannot be resisted by any contrary force or power.

When God's faith is imparted to the believer, and His irresistible power is unleashed, violent things begin to happen in the form of radical changes and victories. God has imparted His righteousness to you. By the stripes of Jesus you were healed. You have been set free. You are perfect in Christ. There is no need to keep on struggling even though tough times are coming – not if you know how to unleash God's irresistible faith.

God simply wants you and me to be vessels He can use. The faith and the power don't belong to us; they belong to Him. Our job is to let His faith and power go, flow, and grow – to release and unleash the miracle-working power of God wherever we go.

He wants us to win the lost and to minister to those in trouble of all sorts. He equips us to do this with His irresistible faith and power.

Submit to God

The Body of Christ also needs to come into submission to God. The prophet Jeremiah wrote, "Thus says the Lord: 'Cursed is the man who trusts in man and makes flesh his strength, whose heart departs from the Lord. For he shall be like a shrub in the desert, and shall not see when good comes, but shall inhabit the parched places in the wilderness, in a salt land which is not inhabited. Blessed is the man who trusts in the Lord, and whose hope is the Lord. For he shall be like a tree planted by the waters, which spreads out its roots by the river, and will not fear when heat comes, but its leaf will be green, and will not be anxious in the year of drought, nor will cease from yielding fruit" (Jeremiah 17:5-8).

In this passage God paints a powerful contrast between the submitted life of a believer and the life of one who forsakes God's ways. He warns us to not trust in man, the creature. Instead, He wants us to put all of our trust in Him, the Creator.

God will not infringe on our free will. Therefore, if we begin to trust in other created beings or things rather than the Creator Himself, He has to let us go. This is why so many Christians are not leading victorious lives. They are trusting in anything and everything but the One who is completely trustworthy in every respect.

The problems you face do not have to be your burden. In a very real sense, your situations, dilemmas, addictions, fears, and problems belong to God – if you give them to Him. As you learn to release God's faith, you will see positive changes taking place.

Jesus said, "Come to me, all you who labor and are heavy laden, and I will give you rest" (Matthew 11:28). That promise still holds true today.

Many secular recovery programs require people to attend their meetings every night of the week for the first ninety days or so, but when people are saved we condition them to think that their deliverance will be ensured if they attend church once a week! What's wrong with this picture? It's almost as if people would sooner trust in man (and man-made programs) than in God. Many will attend AA meetings every night, but some Christians resist going to church more than once a week. It is impossible to release the faith of God if we place our trust predominantly in people rather than in God, as the prophet Jeremiah pointed out.

All Authority

When you asked Jesus Christ to come into your life in order to be your Lord and Savior, you did so with all your heart, and He responded by immediately coming into your heart. The entire, triune God came into you, and He now dwells within you.

You don't walk only with Jesus, or with the Holy Spirit, or with the Father. You walk with all three. The power of God is within you. Jesus said, "All authority has been given to Me in heaven and on earth" (Matthew 28:18). The One who possesses all authority in heaven and in earth has taken up residence within you, and that means that all power and authority in heaven and earth now dwell within you too. That's a stunning thought!

Therefore, the anointing is within you as well as upon you. In Old Testament times, the anointing was available only for prophets, kings, and judges. It was a limited anointing in those days, but this is no longer true. The anointing is for everyone who invites Jesus to come into their life. When Jesus comes into our hearts, the anointing comes in as well. Because His Spirit dwells within you, His anointing is within you as well.

Many people today would rather turn to a pill than to the anointing. Some would go to the alcohol bottle for courage rather than the anointing. Others look to education to provide the answers rather than the anointing. Still others go to psychiatrists and psychologists instead of going to the anointing. Whenever we lean on something other than God, we will surely fail. The Bible says, "Trust in the Lord with all your heart; and lean not on your own understanding. In all your ways acknowledge Him, and He shall direct your paths" (Proverbs 3:5-6). *Violent faith* seizes this truth and realizes that this is all we really need to know.

God says that you are under the curse if you are trusting in man, and He says that He cannot bless you when you are trusting in the arm of flesh. The anointing of the Holy Spirit is accessed when you unleash the faith of God.

People around us are dying without a Savior, and even Christians are dying of Satan-bred diseases. These circumstances are not God's will. God doesn't want people to come to destruction. He surely does not want His people to be destroyed. It is the enemy who brings destruction to people's lives, health, finances, and families.

Jesus said, "The thief does not come except to steal, and to kill, and to destroy. I have come that they may have life, and that they may have it more abundantly" (John 10:10). It is clear that God wants us to experience His abundant life and victory, and the way to appropriate these blessings is to release the faith of God that He has imparted to us.

But our loving Father wants more from His people than having them simply sitting around in "bless-me clubs," listening to nice music and messages. He wants us to get involved in the ministry of the gospel of Jesus Christ, because it is "the power of God to salvation for everyone who believes" (Romans 1:16). In the same way that the power of God's salvation comes to us through faith, so does every other blessing He has in store for us.

At our meetings at Victory in Jesus we are able, through *violent faith*, to release the power of God on behalf of the handicapped, cancer patients, AIDS victims, alcoholics, and drug addicts. But I don't want anyone to look to me for help and healing – it's all God. He uses me to activate His power in our services in order to minister to the real needs of others.

61

You and I are simply vehicles through which the power of God is unleashed. What a privilege that is! We don't have to do a whole lot – just exercise the *violent faith* He imparts to us – and He simply flows through us. It's an exciting way to see results in ministry.

Because God is a Spirit, He needs us – physical entities – in which and through which to manifest Himself. That is why He made us. Therefore, it's vitally important for each of us to learn how to unleash the power of God.

If you venture into ministry without this kind of faith, you will do people an injustice because you simply don't know how to release the power of God on their behalf. In that case, you would be better off not praying over people at all rather than praying in a powerless way. You should not even lay hands on people unless you know how to release God's power into the situation.

No Substance

When a believer learns how to release the power of God through *violent faith*, situations that once seemed overwhelmingly troublesome become like shadows without a substance. The situations may continue to exist, but your ability to cope with them and your point of view have changed. The devil and his henchmen will always try to remind you of them, but when you learn how to release God's power in the midst of the situation, you can immediately experience victory over the evil one and his fiery darts of wickedness.

When troubling thoughts come into our minds, it is our job to shut the door on them. In fact, we should slam the door and bolt it shut! The devil may tempt you to think negative thoughts. When that happens, take positive action immediately by first of all recognizing that those thoughts are from the devil. Secondly, remember that he is a liar, an accuser, and a deceiver. Next, release God's power through *violent faith* – and slam the door.

Once in a while I find myself counseling people who forget that the power of God can change any situation. They might say to me, "You just don't know my husband; he'll never change." It's as though the individual has traded the power of God for hopelessness. That's not a good deal.

God knows every person He has created. He knows what makes them tick, and He knows what they need. Therefore, no person and no situation is ever hopeless.

There are people in the Body of Christ who have opened the door to Satan and closed the door to God. Usually, of course, they don't realize that this is what they've done, but it is true nonetheless. They have closed the door to the power of God, because they've listened to the thoughts of the enemy.

Multitudes of Christians are suffering in horrible situations because they've closed the door on God and have opened the door to Satan. They've chosen to believe a lie.

There's only one way to win – through faith. The Bible says, "For whatever is born of God overcomes the world. And this is the victory that overcomes the world – our faith" (1 John 5:4).

Dwell on God

The prophet Isaiah wrote, "I am the Lord, who makes all things, who stretches out the heavens alone, who spreads abroad the earth by Myself ; who frustrates the signs of the babblers, and drives diviners mad; who turns wise men backward, and makes their knowledge foolishness; who confirms the word of His servant, and performs the counsel of His messengers" (Isaiah 44:24-26).

Maybe you're thinking, *But I don't know the Bible. I haven't memorized any verses. How can I possibly speak the words that will make the enemy flee?* Isaiah tells us that God will confirm the words of His servants and perform the counsel of His messengers. That's all we need to remember. Then, as we study Scripture, we will find Paul's words to Timothy coming true in our lives: "Be diligent to present yourself approved to God, a worker who does not need to be ashamed, rightly dividing the word of truth" (2 Timothy 2:15).

When you say, "Devil, get out of my life" with the voice of authority that comes from God's *violent faith*, he will flee, because God's Word promises this to us. Speak the truth with the authority that comes from knowing who God is. Speak words of life with confidence in your God. You have nothing to lose and everything to gain, because God promises that He will confirm your words as well as His own.

When you speak the Word of God, you antagonize the devil, because, as Jesus said, "It is the Spirit who gives life; the flesh profits nothing. The words that I speak to you are spirit, and they are life" (John 6:63).

Build up your faith through the Word of God. We are already victorious; we don't have to wait for the victory. The victory is ours already. The victory is won.

It all depends on us and our walk with God. God always knows what we are going through, and He cares. He looks at the way we handle the situations that come our way. He wants to see if we will walk away from the problem by turning our back on it and going in His direction.

Dwell on God, not on the difficulty. Don't worry about the members of your family; give them to God. Don't try to control them either; let God break through to them.

When I surrendered my children to God, He saved them, and now He's using them in the building of His kingdom. God moves in when we shut the door behind us, slamming it tightly against the situations of life and opening up to all God has for us.

Circumstances Are Not Your Master

Move by faith against the circumstances that oppose you, and God will see you through. Move with doubt against the same circumstances, and God cannot help you. When you move by faith, you deny the flesh and put demands on God. God does not expect us to demand things of Him, but He will respond to our faith.

When you go to the dentist to have a tooth removed, the process seems frightening because of the probability of pain. The dentist uses a needle to put your mind at rest, because a shot of Novocaine will do the necessary work without any pain to you. At first, you may sit in the chair with your hands gripping the end of the arm and your knuckles turning white. Fear is at work.

However, you know the dentist will inject you with a pain-killer, and once you get over the fear of the needle, you are able to experience the rest that comes from knowing the medication will protect you from pain. That frees the dentist to do the necessary work.

It's the same with God. When you let go, and let Him do His work, He is able to move in your behalf. He is able to keep you from the pain and anguish you fear. He can accomplish great things in and through the life of one who surrenders all to Him.

Come to God. Realize that He loves you. Recognize Him to be the great burden-bearer of your life. Deny the flesh and deny the self-life, and the Holy Spirit will take care of you. He wants to, because He loves you.

Eight

MIXING THE WORD WITH FAITH

*"For indeed the gospel was preached to
us as well as to them; but the word preached
did not profit them, not being mixed with faith in
those who heard it."* *(Hebrews 4:2)*

A Higher Reality

The world of the five physical senses is a real
world, but there is a higher reality than that – the
spiritual realm. Few people, including some believers,
realize the importance of this. There is a clear
distinction between the spiritual and natural worlds.
The devil, our abominable adversary, knows the
difference, but many people do not understand it. This
is why some people try to stifle the word of faith when
they hear it preached.

The enemy of our souls knows that a believer
who is acting on faith is a true threat to him and his
kingdom of darkness. In fact, such a believer is one of
the few threats he faces. That's because the devil is a
spirit, and the only way we can come against him is
through faith – *violent faith* that overthrows him and
his legions.

We are only occupying this natural world for a brief time. It is almost an illusion. The greater reality is spiritual in nature, and faith enables us to find that higher dimension of life in God. We are on this plane – the earthly plane – for only a short time. We will be in the spiritual realm forever. Therefore, spiritual issues demand our time, our energy, our all.

The Word tells us that the things we see are temporal, but the things we cannot see are eternal (see 2 Corinthians 4:18). This clearly shows us that our time and talents should focus on eternal things rather than temporal things.

Medical science may think it's on the brink of finding a way for a person to live in the natural world forever, but that's not going to happen. *Everything* will pass away except the Word of God, which will endure forever.

The devil is a liar. He tries to convince people, especially young people, that they won't die. There is a physical death, but believers will not have to feel the sting of death, as the Apostle Paul declares, "O death, where is your sting? O Hades, where is your victory? The sting of death is sin, and the strength of sin is the law. But thanks be to God, who gives us the victory through our Lord Jesus Christ" (1 Corinthians15:55-57).

It is *violent faith* that enables us to receive this promise. *Violent faith* enables us to confront the last enemy, which is death, and to overthrow death with real spiritual power. People like to say, "You can't get out of this life alive." But, for the believer, the rapture provides a way to "get out of this life alive," and I believe many of us will be privileged, blessed and glorified to experience the rapture in the very near future.

Death Without Hope

We are living in extremely perilous times. Many people seem to be adrift on a sea of doubt and confusion. Judeo-Christian values have fallen victim to a morality based on unbiblical principles. It is a frightening time to be alive, because even Christians are compromising their values.

People in the world are dying foolishly. They are dying without Christ and without hope. When a person dies without Christ, he or she will not see the kingdom of God. Jesus told us that we would not see the kingdom of God unless we are born again. When Nicodemus confronted Him, Jesus answered, "Unless one is born of water and the Spirit, he cannot enter the kingdom of God" (John 3:5).

Violent Faith Brings Revival

We cannot have true spiritual revival without *violent faith*. When God is ready to bring revival, we have to be ready too, and faith is the preparation for revival. We can apprehend and understand spiritual realities only by faith.

Are we, as the Body of Christ, ready to minister to the souls that the end-time harvest brings to us? Are we ready to equip new believers with *violent faith*?

Without faith, we cannot possibly please our Father. Without faith, we cannot be victorious. Without faith, we cannot claim God's promise. The most unfortunate people in the world are the people without faith. The fortunate people in the world are those who know how to apply their faith in every situation.

The Book of Hebrews warns: "For indeed the gospel was preached to us as well as to them; but the word preached did not profit them, not being mixed with faith in those who heard it" (Hebrews 4:2). The Word is of no profit to a person who is without faith. In many churches, even though the Word is preached, it is not mixed with faith. Therefore, it has absolutely no power. Faith is the power that activates the Word. Faith enables the Word to do its powerful work in our lives.

Once, when I was preaching in a prison, I asked the inmates, "How many of you were brought up in denominational churches?" One hundred percent of the inmates raised their hands. I then asked, "Well, how did you end up here?"

It was a rhetorical question. I wanted to point out to them that even though they had heard the Word preached, it had probably not been mixed with faith. When the Word is mixed with faith, powerful things happen.

Many people went to Sunday school when they were little. They loved Jesus, as they understood Him to be. They learned Bible verses and shared the verses they memorized in front of large groups. But in all too many cases, the Word was not mixed with faith, resulting in a weak and emaciated Christian.

The Book of Proverbs says, "Train up a child in the way he should go, and when he is old he will not depart from it" (Proverbs 22:6). This promise is forever true, and it is a word that every believing parent can hold on to. Many of us went to church and Sunday school – we were "trained up." We loved Jesus, and we believed in Him, but then what happened to us? In a sense, we were "trained up" in the way we should go, but because the Word was not mixed with faith – either in us or in the adults around us

– we were sidetracked into thinking and living according to this world's standards.

When the gospel of Jesus Christ is preached in faith, it is received with faith. *Violent faith* is the essential ingredient.

Unlimited Faith

When the gospel is preached with faith, dynamic things happen. Feelings have nothing to do with it. Paul wrote, "For I am not ashamed of the gospel of Christ, for it is the power of God to salvation for everyone who *believes*" (Romans 1:16, italics mine). Notice how the power and faith are intertwined. There can be no true spiritual power without faith.

The devil knows that if he can keep God's people away from faith, he has won. That's why people who started out by learning about Christ may end up in turmoil and confusion. Some find themselves involved with alcohol, drugs, and other addictions. The Word of God that they heard as children was not mixed with faith.

God's faith is unlimited in its power and its scope. Faith is able to put down any situation that comes against you. Faith has no limitations – no time limits or power limitations. Faith simply believes the Word of God.

Evil is evil. When evil thoughts come into your mind, you immediately know by the Word of faith that the voice within you is a liar's voice, and you come against it with the power of *violent faith.* When the gospel is preached in faith or the Word is read in faith, the result is unlimited power.

Why should we permit the devil to humiliate us when we should be humiliating him? When we truly believe the promises of God's Word, we know that the devil is a defeated foe.

Courage Amid Discouragement

There is a place in God where worry is no longer in a believer's vocabulary. There is a place where courage overcomes all odds and applied faith works. It's an exciting place to be.

People cannot steal your faith, but they can undermine it by trying to discourage you and put you down. The devil uses such people to get you to worry so that you will fail to act on your faith. Faith is not a reasonable thing. Faith does not operate according to the standards of this world. Faith does not have to be logical.

When you start acting on faith, you become a threat to the devil and to every tactic he uses to try to defeat you. God will take care of everything if you will surrender everything to Him. Whether it's a slight headache or a malignant tumor, God will take care of it. Your role is to cooperate with Him through faith.

Nine

FROM FAITH TO FAITH

*For in it the righteousness of God is revealed from faith
to faith; as it is written, "The just shall live by faith."*
(Romans 1:17)

Releasing the Power

This is *violent faith* – the faith of God – the kind
of faith that releases great power under the anointing
of the Holy Spirit. What are the keys to releasing this
faith in any given situation?

1. Have the faith of God. This is already our
possession because of grace. The new birth assures us
that we have God's faith, and the Holy Spirit within us
anoints God's faith with power.

2. Speak the faith of God. Remember how David
prophetically spoke forth the outcome of his battle with
Goliath? We must do the same by faith, no matter how
high the mountain or tall the giant seems to be.

3. Take authority. When God created human
beings, it was His plan that we should take authority
over all creation. He intended for us to be victors, not
victims. *Violent faith* enables us to take dominion over
every circumstance through the power of the Holy
Spirit.

4. Do not doubt. There is no place for doubt in a believer's heart. As members of the body of Christ, we are believers, not doubters. In fact, we *know* that nothing is impossible with God.

5. Believe. The gospel chorus says it well: "Only believe, only believe; all things are possible – only believe." In the kingdom of God, to believe is to receive.

6. Receive. The key to receiving is believing. When you operate in the wonderfully exciting realm of *violent faith*, you will possess what you confess. You will own what you utter, and you will receive what you believe.

7. Pray with faith. God hears and answers the prayer of faith. "But without faith it is impossible to please Him, for he who comes to God must believe that He is, and that He is a rewarder of those who diligently seek Him" (Hebrews 11:6).

Many people in the Body of Christ are praying under the anointing, but they don't know how to release the power. The same authority and anointing that were upon David is available to us today, and it makes us winners. We can't lose when we are operating in the realm of *violent faith*. In the same way that David acted on something that had been implanted deep within him while he was in his mother's womb, we can release God's great power in any given situation, and the results are always glorious when we do.

The Greatest Power in the World

When demonic powers of darkness see the anointing and the power within a believer, they become fearful, especially if they sense that the believer knows how to operate in the realm of God's almighty power that comes through the faith that is by Him.

When we release the inherent power we have through the Holy Spirit, God is greatly pleased. He is always pleased when we express faith and live by faith. Essentially, this powerful process comes about in several all-important steps:

- We act on the faith within us. This pleases God.
- The Holy Spirit within us responds to God's faith. This is the anointing and the power.
- The faith of God is released. This is the reward God gives to our faith.

This is simply a God-given ability. As Peter pointed out, "As each one has received the gift, minister it to one another, as good stewards of the manifold grace of God" (1 Peter 4:10). Peter goes on to say, "If anyone speaks, let him speak as the oracles of God. If anyone ministers, let him do it as with the ability which God supplies, that in all things God may be glorified through Jesus Christ" (1 Peter 4:11).

Spontaneous Power

The anointing is the weapon of God. It is the source of the believer's power. When we become familiar with this power, it becomes natural and spontaneous to us. Nancy, my wife, once ministered to a bus driver who told her he was going through a battle with colon cancer. Nancy seized this opportunity to let the anointing do its work, and she cursed the cancer at its roots (as Jesus did with the fig tree). Then she commanded that it come out of his body harmlessly.

The bus driver said, "I hope this is true. I'm scheduled for surgery tomorrow." Nancy boldly confronted the cancer, in front of a bus full of unbelievers, in the *violent faith* of God. It was spontaneous and natural for her to do this.

A few weeks later, she boarded a city bus driven by the man she had prayed for. He was glorifying God spontaneously and naturally. He said, "When I went to the hospital they couldn't find the cancer!" He was so excited and grateful that tears streamed down his face.

Nancy knew the power that comes from the anointing, so she flowed with it naturally and spontaneously. To others on the bus it must have seemed strange, if not alarming, but to Nancy it was just a normal part of a day's experience.

If we don't become familiar with the power of the anointing by flowing with it, it will never become spontaneous to us. Indeed, we are commanded to live by this kind of faith.

In Hebrews 11 – God's great "Faith Hall of Fame" – we see what happens when people operate according to the faith of God. Faith enables us to see. Faith has substance. It is real, and it is vital.

God always rewards faith. Faith enabled Enoch to be translated and Noah and his family to be saved. It led Abraham to the Promised Land. Through faith, Sarah conceived a child at an advanced age. It empowered the great patriarchs – Isaac, Jacob, Joseph, Moses – and later, David, to be victorious in all circumstances. It is the same faith that is available to believers today.

From Our Faith to God's Faith

Paul wrote "For in it the righteousness of God is revealed from faith to faith; as it is written, 'The just shall live by faith" (Romans 1:17). I believe Paul is showing that God wants us to move from our faith (fruit-of-the-Spirit faith), which is within us, to the faith of God (*violent faith*).

Our faith explodes as we get the Word of God into us. As our faith is built up, we begin to live in it. Through this process we begin to live our faith.

We need to remember that *violent faith* is far greater than any other violence or power in the world. As the Word becomes part of us – deep within us – we speak it forth, and great power is unleashed.

Paul wrote, "But what does it say? 'The word is near you, in your mouth and in your heart' (that is, the word of faith which we preach): that if you confess with your mouth the Lord Jesus and believe in your heart that God has raised Him from the dead, you will be saved. For with the heart one believes unto righteousness, and with the mouth confession is made unto salvation. For the Scripture says, 'Whoever believes on Him will not be put to shame' "(Romans 10:8-11).

The Word of faith is within us. When we speak it, faith comes forth. When linked together, the power of the Word of God and the power of the Holy Spirit bring forth miracles. The Bible says, "For the Word of God is living and powerful, and sharper than any two-edged sword, piercing even to the division of soul and spirit, and of joints and marrow, and is a discerner of the thoughts and intents of the heart" (Hebrews 4:12).

Operating in God's Power

When times of drought come, remember that they serve to drive your roots deeper into the soil of God's faith. It is the anointing of the Holy Spirit, not any circumstances in life, that determines your success. Persistence is a way of life for people of faith.

In order to operate in God's power:

- Obey the moving of the Holy Spirit. "For if you live according to the flesh you will die; but if by the Spirit you put to death the deeds of the body, you will live. For as many as are led by the Spirit of God, these are sons of God" (Romans 8:13-14).

- Live according to the Word of God and speak forth its truth. "Now this is the confidence that we have in Him, that if we ask anything according to His will, He hears us. And if we know that He hears us, whatever we ask, we know that we have the petitions that we have asked of Him" (1 John 5:14-15).

- Walk in love. "For in Christ Jesus neither circumcision nor uncircumcision avails anything, but faith working through love" (Galatians 5:6).

When Paul wrote to the young church in Galatia, he stressed the overarching importance of faith. He contrasted observing the law with living by faith. In so doing, he began chapter three with these words: "O foolish Galatians! Who has bewitched you?...Did you receive the Spirit by the works of the law, or by the hearing of faith?" (Galatians 3:2).

Paul reminded them of Abraham's faith and then said, "Therefore know that only those who are of faith are sons of Abraham" (Galatians 3:7). He elaborates further on this all-important truth: "But that no one is justified by the law in the sight of God is evident, for 'the just shall live by faith.' Yet the law is not of faith" (Galatians 3:11-12). The Galatians were convinced that their own goodness was all that was necessary, but Paul persisted in pointing out to them that the law serves only one purpose, and that is to show us how inadequate we are. He pointed out, "But before faith came, we were kept under guard by the law, kept for the faith which would afterward be revealed. Therefore the law was our tutor to bring us to Christ, that we might be justified by faith. But after faith has come, we are no longer under a tutor. For you are all sons of God through faith in Christ Jesus" (Galatians 3:23-26).

It is through faith that we become children of God, and it is by faith that we are justified. It is also by faith that we shall prevail.

This is the *violent faith* that we need today: "For whatever is born of God overcomes the world. And this is the victory that overcomes the world – even our faith" (1 John 5:4).

Taking the Kingdom by Force

Jesus said, "And from the days of John the Baptist until now the kingdom of heaven suffers violence, and the violent take it by force" (Matthew 11:12). This, in my opinion, is a reference to *violent faith* – a faith that seizes the kingdom of God and holds on to it. We must be filled with holy zeal and earnestness as we occupy the kingdom on earth until Jesus returns.

The demons of hell will oppose us in this endeavor, and this demands a violent response on our part. *Violent faith* is violent earnestness, violent perseverance, violent steadfastness, and violent boldness. We must be defiant in our stand against evil.

Sometimes even other believers will oppose us, but we should not let this deter us from the goals of *violent faith* – to keep on fighting the good fight of faith until every enemy is overthrown.

Violent faith gives us great confidence, as David exhibited before Goliath. It knows that no enemy will ever prevail against us. *Violent faith* does not recoil in fear. *Violent faith* always proclaims, "Who shall separate us from the love of Christ? Shall tribulation, or distress, or persecution, or famine, or nakedness, or peril, or sword? As it is written: 'For Your sake we are killed all day long; we are accounted as sheep for the slaughter.' Yet in all these things we are more than conquerors through Him who loved us. For I am persuaded that neither death nor life, nor angels nor principalities nor powers, nor things present nor things to come, nor height, nor depth, nor any other created thing, shall be able to separate us from the love of God which is in Christ Jesus our Lord" (Romans 8:35-39).

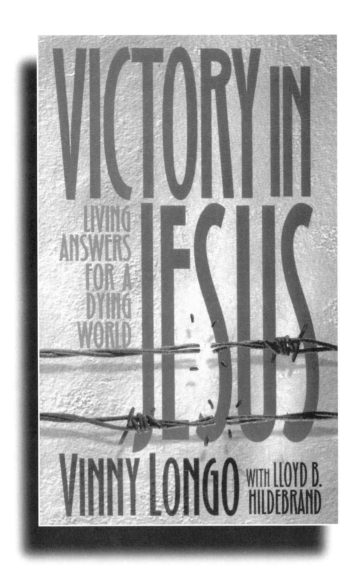

Vinny Longo
is also the author of Victory in Jesus,
available at fine Christian bookstores.